THE FLASH

VOLUME 5
HISTORY LESSONS

BRIAN **BUCCELLATO**
CHRISTOS N. **GAGE**
NICOLE **DUBUC** writers

PATRICK **ZIRCHER** SAMI **BASRI**
NEIL **GOOGE** AGUSTIN **PADILLA**
CULLY **HAMNER** artists

MATT **HOLLINGSWORTH** STELLAR **LABS**
WIL **QUINTANA** MATTHEW **WILSON** colorists

CARLOS M. **MANGUAL** TAYLOR **ESPOSITO**
SAL **CIPRIANO** letterers

PASQUAL **FERRY** & BRAD **ANDERSON**
collection cover artists

BRIAN CUNNINGHAM WIL MOSS Editors – Original Series HARVEY RICHARDS Associate Editor – Original Series
KATE DURRÉ Assistant Editor – Original Series JEB WOODARD Group Editor – Collected Editions
LIZ ERICKSON Editor ROBBIE BIEDERMAN Publication Design

BOB HARRAS Senior VP – Editor-in-Chief, DC Comics

DIANE NELSON President DAN DIDIO and JIM LEE Co-Publishers
GEOFF JOHNS Chief Creative Officer AMIT DESAI Senior VP – Marketing & Global Franchise Management
NAIRI GARDINER Senior VP – Finance SAM ADES VP – Digital Marketing BOBBIE CHASE VP –Talent Development
MARK CHIARELLO Senior VP – Art, Design & Collected Editions JOHN CUNNINGHAM VP – Content Strategy
ANNE DEPIES VP – Strategy Planning & Reporting DON FALLETTI VP – Manufacturing Operations
LAWRENCE GANEM VP – Editorial Administration & Talent Relations ALISON GILL Senior VP – Manufacturing & Operations
HANK KANALZ Senior VP – Editorial Strategy & Administration JAY KOGAN VP – Legal Affairs
DEREK MADDALENA Senior VP – Sales & Business Development DAN MIRON VP – Sales Planning & Trade Development
NICK NAPOLITANO VP – Manufacturing Administration CAROL ROEDER VP – Marketing
EDDIE SCANNELL VP – Mass Account & Digital Sales SUSAN SHEPPARD VP – Business Affairs
COURTNEY SIMMONS Senior VP – Publicity & Communications JIM (SKI) SOKOLOWSKI VP – Comic Book Specialty & Newsstand Sales

THE FLASH VOLUME 5: HISTORY LESSONS

DC Comics, 4000 Warner Blvd. Burbank, CA 91522. A Warner Bros. Entertainment Company.
Printed by RR Donnelley, Owensville, MO, USA. 7/31/15. First Printing

ISBN: 978-1-4012-5772-9

Library of Congress Cataloging-in-Publication Data

Buccellato, Brian.
The Flash. Volume 5, History lessons / Brian Buccellato, Patrick Zircher.
pages cm. — (The New 52!)
ISBN 978-1-4012-5772-9 (paperback)
1. Graphic novels. I. Zircher, Patrick, illustrator. II. Title. III. Title: History lessons.

PN6728.F53B84 2015
741.5'973—dc23

2014033188

THE QUICK AND THE GREEN
BRIAN BUCCELLATO writer SAMI BASRI artist
DETAILS
NICOLE DUBUC writer CULLY HAMNER artist cover art by FRANCIS MANAPUL & BRIAN BUCCELLATO

A FEW YEARS AGO. CENTRAL CITY POLICE LAB.

...IT WAS ALSO A HEARTBREAKING CASE I'LL NEVER FORGET.

CHILDREN WERE DISAPPEARING FROM GROUP HOMES ALL ACROSS THE COUNTRY.

I WAS STILL A RELATIVELY NEW POLICE SCIENTIST, AND AN EVEN NEWER SUPER-HERO.

THERE WAS NO FORENSIC EVIDENCE, NO WITNESSES, AND NOTHING TO EXPLAIN WHO TOOK THESE CHILDREN. THE F.B.I. OPENED A CASE, BUT THEY HAD NO LEADS AND WERE BOGGED DOWN WITH THE USUAL RED TAPE. SO I STARTED MY OWN INVESTIGATION. EXCEPT ALL I HAD TO GO ON WAS THE FEW FACTS OF THE LINKED CASES...

DOZENS OF KIDS WERE DISAPPEARING IN THE MIDDLE OF THE NIGHT...ALWAYS DURING THE FIRST NIGHT OF A LUNAR CYCLE.

AS CHILDREN DISAPPEARED IN PLACES LIKE CENTRAL CITY, SEATTLE AND COAST CITY, I COMPILED THE DATA, LOOKED FOR PATTERNS, AND WAITED.

IT WASN'T UNTIL THE PERPETRATORS STARTED CYCLING BACK TO PREVIOUSLY HIT LOCATIONS THAT I FINALLY CAUGHT A BREAK...

COAST CITY CHILDREN'S HOME.

I DETERMINED WHEN AND WHERE THE KIDNAPPERS WOULD STRIKE NEXT...

...AND WAITED FOR THEM TO SHOW UP.

TURNS OUT, I WASN'T THE ONLY ONE.

YOU LIKE STEALING KIDS?!?

FLASH
OUT OF
WATER

DAMN IT.

VIBRATING
THROUGH SOLID
OBJECTS—IT HAS
ITS ADVANTAGES...

...AND ITS
DRAWBACKS.

AND TO BE HONEST, PART OF ME IS GLAD. THIS IS PERSONAL...

...AFTER WHAT THEY DID TO DR. CARLSON.

THE MAN WORKED WITH DEADLY DISEASES. ANTHRAX, SMALLPOX--YOU NAME IT.

FAR AS WE CAN TELL, IT'S AN ACCIDENT. HE STUMBLES INTO A SHELF OF BEAKERS AND WHATNOT HOLDING ALL THOSE GERMS, THEY BREAK...TRAGIC, BUT NO SIGN OF FOUL PLAY.

BLUE VALLEY. *JUST OUTSIDE OF CENTRAL CITY.*

NORMALLY WE'D GET YOU C.S.I. GUYS IN TO MAKE SURE. FOR OBVIOUS REASONS, THAT'S NOT AN OPTION HERE. AND THE DECONTAMINATION PROCESS IS GONNA DESTROY EVIDENCE.

SO YOU GOTTA DO THE BEST YOU CAN FROM OUT HERE. SORRY ABOUT THAT, ALLEN. I GUESS YOU COULD LOOK AT IT LIKE A CHALLENGE.

I PROBABLY WOULD... IF I DIDN'T *KNOW* THE MAN. DR. CARLSON WAS MY TEACHER, ONE OF MY MAJOR INSPIRATIONS IN BECOMING A FORENSIC SCIENTIST.

AH, HELL. SORRY FOR YOUR LOSS. I CAN CALL SOMEONE ELSE--

NO, I'LL CONSULT WITH A COLLEAGUE, *PATTY SPIVOT,* JUST TO BE THOROUGH. BUT THERE'S NO NEED TO APOLOGIZE. I *WANT* TO BE INVOLVED.

I OWE HIM THAT MUCH.

THE BODY POSITION IS CONSISTENT WITH HIS STUMBLING BACKWARD INTO THE SHELF.

OR BEING *PUSHED*. THERE'S BRUISING ON HIS NECK THAT COULD SUGGEST A STRUGGLE.

IT COULD *ALSO* BE A SYMPTOM OF ONE OF THE PATHOGENS. WITHOUT GETTING IN THERE, WE CAN'T TELL.

I KNOW HE MEANT A LOT TO YOU, BARRY, AND IT'S HARD TO ACCEPT, BUT SOMETIMES TRAGIC ACCIDENTS HAPPEN.

"AND THEY DON'T ALWAYS WORK OUT AS WELL AS *YOURS*."

I REALIZE THAT. BUT DAMN IT, PATTY, HE WAS THE MOST CAREFUL MAN I EVER MET!

WE CAN'T GO INSIDE. BUT IF THERE WAS SOMEONE ELSE HERE, THEY HAD TO GET AWAY SOMEHOW.

IT'S A DIRT ROAD. WITH NO TIRE TRACKS THAT DON'T MATCH DR. CARLSON'S CAR OR OURS.

SOMETHING YOU LEARN IN MY OTHER LINE OF WORK: THERE'S MORE THAN *ONE* WAY TO TRAVEL.

LOOKS LIKE THE KIND OF MARKS THAT WOULD BE MADE BY HELICOPTER LANDING GEAR.

HELICOPTERS AREN'T REQUIRED TO FILE A FLIGHT PLAN. NORMALLY THAT'D GIVE THEM PLENTY OF TIME TO GET AWAY BEFORE WE CAN TRACK THEM.

NORMALLY.

YEAH, I TALKED TO A HELO ABOUT THAT TIME. I HAVE THE I.D. NUMBER HERE.

GREAT. I'M UPLOADING IT TO THE LEAGUE COMPUTERS... AH-HA. IT'S JUST BEEN REPORTED BURNING AND ABANDONED NEAR CENTRAL CITY AIRPORT.

THEY'RE PROBABLY UPGRADING TO SOMETHING FASTER.

JUSTICE LEAGUE DATABASE

THE HELICOPTER WAS STOLEN, OF COURSE, BUT IT'S BEEN USED IN A STRING OF AERIAL ROBBERIES. THE GANG'S LED BY A WOMAN NAMED ESTHER BRYANT, A.K.A. THE SKY PIRATE...

...BEST KNOWN AS *SPITFIRE*.

"SHE'S A FORMER STUNT PILOT. MOTIVATED BY A COMBINATION OF GREED AND THRILL-SEEKING.

"SHE AND HER MEN LIKE A CHALLENGE AS MUCH AS THE MONEY. THEY DON'T JUST PULL HEISTS ON HIGH-VALUE TARGETS...

"...THEY DO IT IN WAYS NO ONE EVER IMAGINED *POSSIBLE.*

"THEY SET THEIR SIGHTS ON OBTAINING LETHAL PATHOGENS. BUT DR. CARLSON RESISTED. IT'S LIKELY THEY DIDN'T GET EVERYTHING THEY WANTED FROM HIM.

"WE HAVE TO ASSUME THEY'LL TRY AGAIN."

FLASH FACT: ALTOSTRATUS CLOUDS ARE COMPOSED OF ICE CRYSTALS. BY VIBRATING HIS FEET IN SUCH A WAY AS TO CREATE EXTREME, LOCALIZED UPDRAFTS, FLASH CAN ATTRACT ENOUGH OF THESE CRYSTALS TO PROVIDE JUST ENOUGH SUBSTANCE TO RUN ON...FOR A VERY SHORT TIME!

THAT WOMAN'S INSANE. NO... JUST **AMORAL**. WHAT SHE DID WAS EMINENTLY LOGICAL. DESIGNED TO GET RID OF ME. KILL ME AT BEST, SLOW ME UP AT MINIMUM.

CAN'T WORRY ABOUT THAT NOW. FIRST PRIORITY IS RETRIEVING THE VIALS.

I'VE PRACTICED THIS OFTEN ENOUGH. FALLING FROM GREAT HEIGHTS IS AN OCCUPATIONAL HAZARD. COMBINING FREE-FLYING TECHNIQUES WITH MY SPEED GIVES ME A PRETTY GOOD DEGREE OF MANEUVERABILITY.

OF COURSE, IT'S ONE THING TO DO IT WITH **GREEN LANTERN** STANDING BY IN CASE SOMETHING GOES WRONG...

...AND ANOTHER WHEN YOU'RE CHASING SMALL GLASS TUBES OF **PLAGUE**.

GOT THEM. NOW THERE'S JUST THE SMALL MATTER OF **LANDING**.

THE AURA THAT PROTECTS ME SHOULD ALSO SHIELD THEM TO A SIGNIFICANT DEGREE.

HERE'S HOPING IT'S ENOUGH.

EVEN WITH ONE ARM OTHERWISE OCCUPIED, I SHOULD BE ABLE TO CREATE ENOUGH LIFT TO GIVE ME A RELATIVELY CONTROLLED DESCENT.

THE TRICK WILL BE NOT CONTROLLING IT TOO MUCH--CONSIDERING I NEED TO GET DOWN FAST...

...WHILE MAKING SURE I DON'T LAND HARD ENOUGH TO BREAK THESE EXTREMELY DELICATE VIALS OF VERY DEADLY SUBSTANCES.

AND... EXHALE.

QUICK STOP TO DROP OFF THE VIALS WITH THE POLICE...EXPLAIN WHAT THEY ARE, SCARING EVERYONE SENSELESS... AND PICK UP SPITFIRE'S TRAIL.

BECAUSE IF THE DAMAGE HER MEN CAUSED TO THE PLANE WAS AS BAD AS I THINK...

IT MAKES PEOPLE DO CRAZY THINGS...

DING-DING-DING-DING-DING-DING-DING-DING-DING

LIKE BREAKING INTO *EVERY* LAST JEWELRY STORE ON THE BLOCK, AND ALERTING THE ENTIRE CITY.

THAT'S NOT JUST GREEDY... THAT'S STUPID.

AT LEAST NO ONE IS HURT OR IN JEOPARDY. SO I CAN CONTINUE ONWARD...

I DON'T NEED A TRAIL OF BREAD-CRUMBS TO KNOW WHO IS BEHIND THESE CRIMES.

A PAIR OF ORNERY CRIMINALS WHO ARE AS GREEDY AS THEY ARE MISMATCHED...

I TOLD YOU WE COULD DIVVY IT UP LATER...

YOU THINK I'M GONNA TRUST *YOU*?!

HEY, BARRY...

...FORREST SAID YOU VOLUNTEERED TO TAKE THE COLD CASE AND FRYE SHOT YOU DOWN. WHAT HAPPENED?

I DON'T KNOW. FOR SOME REASON HE DOESN'T WANT ME INVOLVED.

MAYBE YOU SHOULD TALK TO HIM... FIND OUT WHY.

NO MATTER WHAT OUR RELATIONSHIP OUTSIDE OF WORK IS, DARRYL IS STILL OUR CAPTAIN. I'VE GOT TO RESPECT PROTOCOL, PATTY. IT'S FORREST'S CASE.

ARE YOU SURE YOU'RE OKAY? THE BOYFRIEND I KNOW WOULDN'T GIVE UP SO EASILY.

WOOOOOOSHHH

HOLD THAT THOUGHT...

THE *BROOME HILL BUTCHER'S* TIMELINE? *THAT'S* MORE LIKE THE BARRY I KNOW.

IT'S FORREST'S CASE...BUT THAT DOESN'T MEAN I CAN'T GIVE HIM A HA[ND] AS SOON AS WE G[ET] THE NEW FORENS[IC] REPORTS, I CAN PLACE THEM ON THE TIMELINE...

"...AND I CAN START IDENTIFYING THE VICTIMS."

YOU'VE GOT AT LEAST SIX MURDERS WITHIN THE PAST TEN YEARS. ARE YOU *SURE* IT'S RIGHT?

I DOUBLE-CHECKED-- THE VICTIMS WERE ALL IDENTIFIED THROUGH DENTAL RECORDS...AND I PUT THEM ON THE TIMELINE COINCIDING WITH WHEN THEIR MISSING PERSONS REPORTS WERE ORIGINALLY FILED.

IT DOESN'T MAKE SENSE. HOLLIS HOLDEN HAS BEEN LOCKED UP FOR 20 YEARS.

YOU KNOW WHAT THIS *MEANS?*

HOLDEN COULDN'T HAVE MURDERED THEM ALL.

SO... THERE'S *ANOTHER* KILLER OUT THERE?

DAMN. FRYE'S GONNA HAVE A CONNIPTION.

SHE'S RIGHT. THERE WAS ANOTHER KILLER OUT THERE...

...AND HE WAS RIGHT IN OUR BACKYARD...

Nora Allen

...AT THE SAME TIME THAT MOM WAS KILLED.

...THIS ISN'T YOUR CASE. LEAVE IT *ALONE.*

WHY, DARRYL? THIS COULD BE MY CHANCE TO FIND MOM'S KILLER AND *FINALLY* PROVE MY FATHER'S INNOCENCE.

STOP DOING THIS TO YOURSELF, SON.

YOU DON'T UNDERSTAND. I *NEED* THIS.

ALL I'M ASKING IS FOR YOU TO AUTHORIZE THE EXHUMATION OF DYLAN'S BODY SO I CAN GET A DNA SAMPLE. ONE SAMPLE TO COMPARE WITH EVIDENCE FROM MOM'S CASE...

NO. IT WON'T DO ANY GOOD.

THAT'S EASY FOR YOU TO SAY. SHE WASN'T *YOUR* MOTHER.

NO, SHE WASN'T. BUT I LOVED HER MORE THAN YOU'LL EVER KNOW.

WHAT ARE YOU TALKING ABOUT?

BARRY, I... I WASN'T JUST AN OLD FRIEND...

YOUR MOM AND I... HAD HISTORY.

WHAT?

AFTER ALL THIS TIME... WHY DIDN'T YOU EVER TELL ME?

I'M SORRY. WE CAN TALK ABOUT THAT LATER. RIGHT NOW I NEED YOU TO LISTEN TO ME... THIS GUY DIDN'T KILL NORA.

WHY SHOULD I BELIEVE YOU?

BRIAN BUCCELLATO writers PATRICK ZIRCHER artist cover art by PASQUAL FERRY & BRAD ANDERSON

GEM CITY MUSEUM OF HISTORY AND SCIENCE.

SECURITY

MARSHALL FLETCHER

KRRRESH

IRON HEIGHTS PRISON.

AFTER A QUICK DETOUR TO GIVE PATTY A D.N.A. SAMPLE FROM DEAN'S GRAVE...DEADMAN AND I PAY *HOLLIS HOLDEN* A VISIT TO DETERMINE THE EVIL SPIRIT'S TRUE MOTIVE.

OUR BEST SHOT IS FOR DEADMAN TO POSSESS HOLDEN AND SEE WHAT HE REMEMBERS ABOUT HIS TIME AS THE KEYSTONE KILLER...

THROUGH POSSESSION, DEADMAN CAN ACCESS HOLDEN'S MEMORIES...AND THOSE IMPRINTED BY THE KEYSTONE KILLER.

THE DOWNSIDE OF ACCESSING THOSE MEMORIES IS THAT HE *EXPERIENCES* THEM AS THEY HAPPEN.

"IT'S PRETTY *MESSED UP,* FLASH.

"HE WAS ONCE A MINER NAMED *ULYSSES SUTTER,* WHO LIVED IN MISSOURI WITH HIS FAMILY IN THE MID 1800'S. LIFE WAS HARD AND HE STRUGGLED TO SUPPORT HIS FAMILY.

TO FIND ANSWERS, DEADMAN RELIVES SOME TRULY *HORRIFIC* THINGS. BUT HE FIGHTS THROUGH THE PAIN TO DISCOVER KEY FACTS ABOUT THE KEYSTONE KILLER...

"T THE DAWN OF
HE CALIFORNIA
GOLD RUSH, HE
PARTNERED UP
WITH AN OLD
FRIEND AND SET
OFF TO MAKE HIS
FORTUNE.

"BAD WEATHER
FORCED THEM TO
STOP A COUPLE
HUNDRED MILES
WEST OF MISSOURI...
IN WHAT IS NOW
KEYSTONE CITY.

"UNABLE TO CONTINUE
TO CALIFORNIA, THEY
TOOK UP MINING IN
THE UNCLAIMED LAND.
BUT WEEKS OF LABOR
GOT THEM NOTHING.
WITH WINTER COMING,
FLETCHER LEFT TO
GO BACK HOME.

"HIS PERSEVERANCE
PAID OFF AND HE
DISCOVERED
DIAMONDS.

"FLETCHER,
WORRIED FOR
SUTTER'S SAFETY,
WENT BACK TO THE
CAMP TO TAKE
HIM HOME...

"HE FOUND SUTTER
WITH DIAMONDS
AND ASSUMED THE
WORST... THAT HIS
OLD FRIEND
BETRAYED HIM."

"SUTTER, DESPERATE
TO SUPPORT HIS
FAMILY, STAYED
AND CONTINUED...

"HIS FRIEND
WAS MARSHALL
FLETCHER.

"FLETCHER SAW RED... AND ATTACKED SUTTER.

"HE THEN COLLAPSED THE ENTRANCE TO THE MINE, WITH A HALF-DEAD SUTTER INSIDE.

"SUTTER *STARVED TO DEATH* IN THAT MINE... SPENDING HIS LAST MOMENTS CURSING THE NAME FLETCHER.

"FLETCHER RETURNED TO THE TERRITORY IN THE SPRING, WITH OFFICIAL CLAIMS ON ALL OF THE LAND. AND THE *GEM CITIES* WERE BORN...

I CAME HERE TO TRACE THE GENEALOGY OF MARSHALL FLETCHER. THE IDEA WAS TO CREATE HIS FAMILY TREE WITH **ALL** OF THE BRANCHES.

IN ORDER TO FIND THE KEYSTONE KILLER, I'M GOING TO NEED TO MAP WHO HIS TARGETS ARE... HOWEVER MANY THOUSANDS OF DESCENDANTS THAT INCLUDES.

UNFORTUNATELY, ALL OF THE GENEALOGY RECORDS BEFORE THE YEAR 1989 ARE MISSING.

EVERY LAST ONE OF THEM IS **GONE**.

I SHOULD KNOW. I LOOKED **EVERYWHERE**.

ANY LUCK?

THE RECORDS ARE GONE. AS IF SOMEONE **TOOK** THEM.

WITH THE EXCEPTION OF THE FEW NAMES IN THIS PHONE BOOK, WE HAVE NO WAY OF KNOWING HOW MANY FLETCHER HEIRS ARE OUT THERE. DID YOU FIND ANYTHING ON YOUR END?

I DID... AND IT'S NOT **GOOD**.

THIS KIND OF GHOST IS FUELED BY HATE... WHICH MAKES HIM PRETTY MUCH THE WORST KIND OF EVIL SPIRIT.

IF HE HAS ONE WEAKNESS... IT'S THAT HE CAN ONLY POSSESS PEOPLE FOR A LITTLE WHILE BEFORE HE HAS TO JUMP INTO ANOTHER HOST. WITH ONE **EXCEPTION**. IF HE JUMPS INTO THE BODY OF SOMEONE RELATED TO HIM BY BLOOD.

A SUTTER?

I'M GUESSING THAT SOMEWHERE DOWN THE LINE, HOLLIS HOLDEN WAS A SUTTER.

DEADMAN... WHEN YOU WERE INSIDE HOLDEN, YOU SAW THE HORRIFYING THINGS HE DID.

YOU WANNA KNOW IF I SAW YOUR MOM. NORA ALLEN.

HOW DO YOU KNOW--

SORRY, BARRY... I SAW THINGS WHEN I POSSESSED YOU. JUST LIKE I DID WITH HOLDEN. IN ANSWER TO YOUR QUESTION... I DID SEE WHO HE KILLED.

SHE WASN'T ONE OF THEM.

THAT'S A GOOD THING, RIGHT?

SO YOU KNOW MY SECRET IDENTITY, HUH?

UM, SORRY.

IF IT'S ANY CONSOLATION... I WAS SURPRISED.

BARRY, IT'S PATTY. PICK UP IF YOU CAN...IT'S IMPORTANT. I NEED YOU TO COME TO THE MUSEUM, RIGHT AWAY...

GEM CITY MUSEUM OF HISTORY AND SCIENCE.

"THE BROOME HILL BUTCHER HAS KILLED AGAIN..."

HOW IS THIS EVEN *POSSIBLE*, BARRY? COPYCAT?

I'LL TELL YOU ALL ABOUT IT LATER. RIGHT NOW, I'M TRYING TO FIGURE OUT WHERE HE WILL STRIKE NEXT...

MARSHALL FLETCHER

AND WHY THE HELMET AND AXE WERE STOLEN.

NOSTALGIA, MAYBE?

LISTEN, I KNOW HOW MUCH YOU NEED CLOSURE WITH YOUR MOM... BUT FRYE CALLED ME OUT FOR PULLING EVIDENCE FROM HER CASE.

I'M SORRY... I DIDN'T GET A CHANCE TO COMPARE--

IT'S OKAY. HOLDEN DIDN'T DO IT.

YOU SURE? I HAVEN'T EVEN RUN THE D.N.A. TO SEE IF THERE'S A MATCH--

MARSHA

D.N.A.... *WHAT* D.N.A.?

THE D.N.A.!

MARSHALL FLETCHER'S!

THE PIECES ARE FINALLY **ADDING UP.** WE KNOW THAT THE KEYSTONE KILLER WANTS ALL OF THE FLETCHERS DEAD...

SO I WENT TO RESEARCH HIS GENEALOGY TO GET A LIST OF HIS POTENTIAL VICTIMS. IT SEEMED WEIRD THAT THE PERTINENT RECORDS WERE GONE. **WEIRD,** BUT NOT A COINCIDENCE.

SOMEONE TOOK THEM LONG AGO...LIKELY IN AN EFFORT TO KEEP THE KEYSTONE KILLER FROM **FINDING THEM.** THE KEYSTONE KILLER MUST'VE KNOWN THEY WERE MISSING.

WHEN HE WAS TRYING TO POSSESS ME, HE SAID THAT I COULD "HELP HIM FIND THEM ALL." I ASSUMED HE WAS TALKING ABOUT USING MY **POWERS,** BUT HE SAW INSIDE MY HEAD THE SAME WAY DEADMAN DID...

HE SAW THAT I UNEARTHED HIM LOOKING FOR D.N.A. SAMPLES. HE SAW WHO I AM AND WHAT I DO...

CENTRAL CITY POLICE

AND HE KNOWS I HAVE ACCESS TO THE POLICE DATABASE...

THE KEYSTONE KILLER WAS A NINETEENTH CENTURY MINER NAMED **ULYSSES SUTTER**. HE WAS THE TRUE FOUNDER OF THE GEM CITIES BUT WAS MURDERED BY HIS FRIEND MARSHALL FLETCHER, WHO TOOK EVERYTHING FROM HIM...INCLUDING HIS **LEGACY**.

SUTTER'S HATE FOR FLETCHER WAS SO GREAT THAT HE REFUSED TO LET GO OF THIS WORLD. HIS GHOST-SPIRIT WON'T REST UNTIL HE HAS MURDERED **EVERY LAST DESCENDANT** OF FLETCHER'S.

ONCE SUTTER LEARNED THAT I UNEARTHED HIM LOOKING FOR D.N.A. SAMPLES TO LINK TO MY MOTHER'S KILLER, HE REALIZED HE HAD A NEW WAY TO IDENTIFY HIS PREY. SO HE WENT TO MY OFFICE AND POSSESSED KEVIN, THE NIGHT JANITOR.

BUT INSTEAD OF GETTING HIS INFORMATION AND LEAVING, HE KILLED EVERYONE IN SIGHT...

...THEN ACCESSED THE C.C.P.D.'S DATABASE TO COMPILE A LIST OF PEOPLE WHO HAVE **BIOLOGICAL TIES** TO FLETCHER...MATCHING THEM AGAINST D.N.A. SAMPLES FROM MARSHALL FLETCHER'S CLOTHES THAT HE STOLE FROM THE MUSEUM.

BUT EVEN EVIL SPIRITS HAVE THEIR **LIMITATIONS**. THE KEYSTONE KILLER CAN ONLY POSSESS PEOPLE FOR A SHORT TIME...UNLESS THEY ARE **RELATED** TO HIM BY **BLOOD**.

THAT'S WHY HE WAS FORCED TO JUMP FROM THE JANITOR TO FORREST, WORKING A DOUBLE SHIFT. BEFORE LEAVING THE LAB, HE ACQUIRED AN ALARMING PIECE OF INFORMATION...

D.N.A. - 99.8673% MATCH

FRYE, DARRYL

4575 CARMINE WAY

CAPTAIN FRYE IS HIS LAST KNOWN DESCENDANT. THE MAN WHO PRACTICALLY **RAISED ME** AFTER MY MOM DIED.

...IF HE
...S DARRYL,
...RMANENTLY
...ON EARTH.

4575 CARMINE WAY.

PLEASE, LET ME BE IN
TIME. I DON'T WANT TO
LOSE HIM TOO...

FORREST?!

WHAT DO YOU REMEMBER?

≥NNH≤... THAT THING KILLED BEN... AND EDDIE... IT KILLED *EVERYONE* ON THE NIGHT SHIFT IN THE LAB. THEN IT JUMPED INTO *ME*... BROUGHT ME *HERE*.

BUT DARRYL WASN'T HOME.

IT LEFT ME AND WENT INTO A... A POSTAL WORKER.

YOU'RE NOT EASY TO KEEP UP WITH, FLASHDANCE.

THE KILLER COULD BE *ANYONE* BY NOW. WE'VE LOST HIM.

UNTIL WE FIND CAPTAIN FRYE. HE'S THE KEY.

FORREST, I NEED TO FIND *FRYE.* DO YOU KNOW--

HE LEFT A *NOTE* ADDRESSED TO THE KEYSTONE KILLER.

WHAT? WHAT'D IT *SAY?*

THAT *HE* IS THE LAST LIVING SUTTER, SO THE GHOST *NEEDS* HIM.

FRYE ALSO CHALLENGED HIM TO MEET AT THE SPOT WHERE THEY LAST MET.

SO THIS CAPTAIN IS GONNA DONATE HIS BODY TO HIS PSYCHO-ANCESTOR? I'M NOT FEELING THAT MOVE.

DID IT SAY WHERE?

NO, BUT THEY MUST HAVE HISTORY. IF YOU WANT, I CAN HELP--

THANKS, DETECTIVE.

OR NOT.

BE CAREFUL, FLASH.

KEEPING UP WITH THAT IS GETTING OLD, REAL FAST.

...GETTING TOO OLD FOR THIS...

"NO MEDIA WITHIN 100 YARDS OF THIS SCENE, YOU HEAR ME? AND SOMEONE GET *CAPTAIN FRYE* ON THE PHONE. *NOW.*"

CENTRAL CITY POLICE CRIME LAB.

I TRIED, MA'AM. HE'S NOT PICKING UP.

DAVID, LOOK, AFTER WHAT YOU SAW TONIGHT--YOU SHOULD MAKE YOUR STATEMENT AND GO HOME.

THESE ARE *MY* PEOPLE WHO WERE SLAUGHTERED. I'M GOOD *RIGHT HERE*, CHIEF.

YOU'RE SAYING THAT DARRYL IS *RELATED* TO THE KILLER?

YES, PATTY. AND HE'S HATCHED SOME CRAZY PLAN TO STOP THE KILLER. I NEED TO *FIND HIM* BEFORE THE EVIL SPIRIT POSSESSES HIM *PERMANENTLY.*

HOLD ON-- THIS SPIRIT CAN TAKE OVER ANYONE IN HIS HIS BLOODLINE?!

THE LAST PERSON HE TOOK OVER WAS ARCHIBALD DEAN, AND YOU KNOW HOW *THAT* ENDED UP.

I'M GOING TO GO THROUGH DARRYL'S OLD FILES... SEE IF I CAN FIND THEIR "FIRST MEETING PLACE."

WAIT, BARRY...

ABOUT DARRYL...HE MIGHT BE YOUR *BIOLOGICAL FATHER.*

D.N.A. - 99.8673% MATCH
FRYE, DARRYL

NO YOU DON'T, DARRYL...

NOT ON MY WATCH.

YOU'RE NO SUTTER, FRYE! YOU LIED TO GET ME HERE...

BUT NOW I HAVE ACCESS TO YOUR MEMORIES. A BIG MISTAKE. YOU'RE NOT A SUTTER...

...BUT HE IS!

"...SOME REFLEX KICKED IN AND I *VIBRATED* AT DIFFERENT FREQUENCIES UNTIL IT BROKE YOUR HOLD."

"I DID THE SAME THING TO THE KEYSTONE KILLER, TRAPPING HIM INSIDE ME WHILE STILL MAINTAINING CONTROL OVER MY ACTIONS."

"THAT WAS MY PLAN ALL ALONG... I JUST DIDN'T KNOW WHERE I WAS GOING TO TAKE HIM UNTIL YOU DROPPED THE HOUSE OF MYSTERY INTO OUR LAPS."

"YOU PROVIDED ME WITH THE PERFECT PRISON, DEADMAN."

"I OWE YOU ONE."

IS HE...?

HE'S GONE, CAPTAIN FRYE.

"I'M SORRY, BARRY..."

IT'S OKAY, DARRYL. I KNOW YOU DESTROYED THE LINEAGE RECORDS AND DOCTORED THE D.N.A. RESULTS SO IT WOULD LOOK LIKE *YOU* WERE THE LAST DESCENDANT OF THE KILLER INSTEAD OF ME.

YOU WERE TRYING TO PROTECT ME.

SO *YOU* ARE RELATED TO SUTTER, BUT DARRYL ISN'T?

HE'S NOT MY BIOLOGICAL FATHER, PATTY.

ALWAYS THOUGHT THE AY WOULD COME WHEN THE KEYSTONE KILLER WOULD RETURN. I PREPARED FOR IT AS BEST I COULD.

I DID THINGS THAT WERE AGAINST DEPARTMENT *PROTOCOL.* I'VE KNOWINGLY *BROKEN LAWS* IN AN EFFORT TO MAKE SURE THAT HISTORY DOESN'T REPEAT ITSELF.

I HAVE TRADED MY *INTEGRITY* FOR THE SAFETY OF SOMEONE I CONSIDER MY *SON.* I DO NOT REGRET MY CHOICES. BUT I LAMENT MY FAILURES...

I LOVED YOUR MOTHER BEFORE YOU WERE *BORN,* BARRY. I SHOULD'VE TOLD YOU THAT.

BUT THE TIMING NEVER WORKED...AND IT WASN'T MEANT TO BE. SO I LOVED HER FROM AFAR...AND WHEN THE UNTHINKABLE HAPPENED... WITH HER AND YOUR FATHER...

I DID WHAT I HAD TO AND RAISED YOU AS BEST I COULD.

I ALWAYS WANTED NORA IN MY LIFE... AND GOT THAT THROUGH YOU.

I LOVE YOU, SON.

LOVE YOU TOO, DARRYL.

I'M SORRY, TOO. MY PURSUIT OF MOM'S KILLER RESULTED IN ALL OF THIS TRAGEDY. AND I HAVE TO LIVE WITH WHAT SINGH AND FORREST WERE PUT THROUGH...

YOU CAN'T BLAME YOURSELF. HOW COULD YOU KNOW WHAT WOULD HAPPEN?

VARIANT COVER GALLERY

THE FLASH #27
Scribblenauts variant cover by John Katz after Carmine Infantino

THE FLASH #28
Variant cover by Howard Chaykin & Jesus Aburto

THE FLASH #29
Robot Chicken variant cover by RC Stoodios